GW01459399

French

Christmas Cookbook

& Travel Guide
2025/2026

Festive Recipes, Holiday Markets & Winter
Escapes in Paris, Strasbourg, Alsace & Beyond

Melissa S. Wright

Table of Contents

Chapter 1: Noël à la Française: The Spirit of a French Christmas

1.1 The Meaning of Christmas in France.

If you arrive in France in mid-December, you'll feel it before you see it: the subtle buzz of expectation that permeates boulangeries, the faint aroma of orange peel and spice in the air, and the glimmer of fairy lights reflected in café windows. Christmas here isn't raucous or rushed. It emerges slowly, like a narrative repeated every year, held together by food, religion, and family.

You could be asked to join a Parisian family for le Réveillon, the big, late-night feast that follows midnight mass. The evening starts quietly, with glasses of Champagne and platters of saline oysters, fines de claire from **Marennes-Oléron or Belon,** glittering on crushed ice. Someone hands around blinis covered with crème fraîche and salmon, while a youngster snatches a macaron off the dessert dish. The topic moves from politics to pastries, with laughter rising like bubbles in a glass. Around midnight, lights flicker as the family walks to mass at the nearby église, where songs resound under stone vaults still chilly from the winter air.

In Provence, Christmas seems older and slower, steeped in tradition and fragrant with rosemary. Les santons are hand-painted clay sculptures that depict not just the birth narrative but also village life: the baker with his baguette, the shepherd, and the lavender merchant. On Christmas Eve, the table is set for *le Gros Souper,* a Lenten-style dinner of seven modest dishes consumed before midnight, followed by the treize desserts, a festive array of sweets depicting Christ and the twelve apostles. You can taste almonds, figs, nougat, candied orange peel, and a piece of pompe à l'huile, a fragrant olive-oil brioche with hints of orange blossom. The tastes are basic yet holy.

In Alsace, Christmas starts early, frequently on December 6th, when children lay their shoes by the fireplace for Saint Nicholas. They wake up to discover tangerines, chocolates, and mannala–small vanilla-scented brioche guys. Towns like Strasbourg, Colmar, and Kaysersberg are transformed into fairytale settings, with half-timbered buildings hung with lights and market booths offering bredele biscuits in every shape and size. Evenings are for vin chaud infused with cinnamon and star anise, as well as a stroll through gold and red-lit neighborhoods. You can't help but observe how the cold draws people together: cuddled beneath awnings, hands wrapped around hot drinks, smiling at strangers.

Christmas is a common rite across France—not a show, but an intimate rhythm. It may be discovered in the silence before grace, in the way bread is handed around the table, or in the dazzle of tinsel against a windowpane. Whether in a metropolitan flat or a stone farmhouse, Noël in France focuses on little, significant moments that may be tasted, touched, and remembered long after the candles have burnt low.

1.2 A Brief History of French Christmas Traditions.

The tale of Christmas in France predates the tinsel and lights; it is a tapestry made from religion, folklore, and gastronomy that has evolved gradually over the years.

It originated in the Middle Ages, when mystères, the earliest nativity plays, were staged on church steps across France. Actors reenacted Christ's birth while vendors outside sold roasted chestnuts, wine, and wool scarves. By the 13th century, these performances had evolved into yearly communal festivals — part religious liturgy, half village fair — laying the groundwork for the exuberant celebrations that characterize French Christmas today.

During the 15th and 16th centuries, the southern areas of Provence and Languedoc established distinct traditions. Les santons, the little clay figures you see at market stalls today, were initially manufactured in Marseille during the French Revolution, when public nativity displays were outlawed in churches. The people just transported the holy home. They used recognizable figures — the fisherman, miller, and washerwoman — to make each crèche a mirror of their own village life.

In the north and east, Saint Nicolas ruled dominantly. On December 6th, youngsters laid their wooden clogs near the fire, expecting to awaken to sweets and nuts. His mysterious companion, Le Père Fouettard, was thought to chastise misbehavers, serving as a stark reminder that virtue and giving are the season's twin foundations. Père Noël, a softer character clothed in crimson, emerged in the late 19th century, influenced by folklore and popular depiction. By the 1950s, he had supplanted Saint Nicolas in the majority of France; however, the elder saint continues to preside in Alsace and Lorraine.

The French Yule log (Bûche de Noël) has its own history. Long before patisseries developed the rolled sponge and buttercream, families would burn a real log in the fireplace to represent regeneration and light during the darkest hours. The ashes were kept to bless the next year's crop. When central heating replaced open flames, bakers turned the emblem into something edible: a cake that transported the heat of the hearth to the dessert table. Today, the 2025 pâtisserie scene has elevated that history to art, with bûches coated in chestnut cream, garnished with gold foil, or filled with mango-passionfruit mousse from Paris to Lyon.

Meanwhile, public Christmas markets can be traced back to ***Strasbourg's Christkindelsmärik in 1570,*** which is still Europe's oldest, and were founded on a combination of religion and business. What was originally a market selling nativity items and sweets has evolved into a large maze of wooden chalets and illuminated booths, now stocked with sustainable crafts and regional delicacies. In 2025, numerous markets, from Reims to Metz, will stress handcrafted items and eco-friendly décor, showing a contemporary French concern for sustainability even during celebrations.

Despite decades of change, the essence of a French Christmas remains the same: it is an act of gathering. Whether at a church altar, a family table, or a market stall, the season is a ritual of light shared in the dark — a celebration of community and taste that connects past and the present.

1.3 Seasonal Symbols & Stories

If you walk through a Provençal village in December, you'll notice more than just the smell of roasted chestnuts and the sound of church bells. You'll notice the subtle, sensitive elements that give French Christmas its soul: a handmade crèche (nativity scene) lighting in a window, wooden figurines of shepherds and farmers, and maybe, hidden among them, a fisherman or baker – common peasants representing thankfulness for daily life. This is more than simply decorating; it's narrative in clay and color.

The bûche de Noël, a thick, rolling sponge cake swirled with buttercream, originated from the Yule log, which was burned to protect the house from bad spirits and guarantee a bountiful crop. Families used to congregate around the crackling fire, throwing wine or holy water over the log and reciting their wishes for the next year. Today, you can experience the same warmth in each mouthful of chocolate ganache, a contemporary ritual that echoes an old one.

In contrast to the North Pole Santa, Père Noël comes with calm dignity rather than great fanfare. Children leave polished shoes by the fireplace and return in the morning to discover oranges, sugared almonds, and little toys – simple pleasures buried in memories. In Alsace, he is still shadowed by the austere Père Fouettard, a relic of medieval morality stories who reminds you that French folklore is never all sweetness—it is complex, real, and honest.

Les Treize Desserts, a table-long presentation of Christ and his disciples, reignites the richness of Provence. You can practically smell the figs, almonds, and nougat from here – a scene of wealth and trust. Each region's emblems tell a unique tale, much like an embroidered tablecloth handed down through generations. As you unwrap them one by one, you realize that a French Christmas is more about connection than spectacle – to tradition, family, and taste.

1.4 How France Celebrates Today, 2025/2026 Edition

Walk around France in December 2025 and you'll witness a nation that simultaneously honors and reinvents its traditions with calm brilliance. Paris now lights up with more than just glittering displays; energy-efficient LED installations tell visual stories along the Champs-Élysées, with each arrondissement curating its own "green illumination." Strasbourg's famous Christmas Market — the Christkindelsmärik — has returned stronger than ever, emphasizing local artisans, wooden toys, and zero-plastic stalls. Even the mulled wine is served in recyclable stoneware cups that guests may return or keep as keepsakes.

In 2025, the rhythm of Noël has transformed gently and elegantly. More French families travel inside the nation, preferring small Alpine chalets, Loire Valley châteaux, or even canal-side stays in Colmar over long-distance excursions. Sustainability is not a term; it is an instinct. Many towns now hold "slow Christmas" activities such as candlelight markets, choir nights, and seasonal tasting meals with local products.

You will also note how technology improves the experience without dominating it. Digital Advent calendars from Parisian chocolatiers let you virtually taste flavors before purchase, while augmented reality nativity trails in Lyon and Dijon take families through historic lanes.

Yet, at its core, the celebration remains intimate: oysters and champagne on Christmas Eve, laughing that lasts until midnight, and the distinct smells of roasting capon or boiling chestnut soup. The French Noël of 2025/2026 has developed, but its core remains the same: sharing pleasure, generosity, and conviviality at the table and beyond.

Chapter 2 - Winter Escapes in France:

Cities, Villages, and Market Magic

2.1 Paris in December: Lights, Pastries, and Chic Festivals

The first thing you notice is the fragrance of roasted chestnuts wafting over the Champs-Élysées, not the Eiffel Tower. December in Paris sparkles not from the lights, but from the peaceful delight of people gathering over chocolat

chaud, scarves wrapped tightly, and violins echoing under the Seine bridges. Paris in 2025 is a lesson in winter elegance—refined, sensorial, and effortlessly joyous.

At the Tuileries Garden Christmas Market, rows of wooden chalets now house entrepreneurs that specialize in sustainability, such as locally created candles, eco-wool scarves, and fair-trade chocolates. The "Green Paris Noël" campaign reduces single-use plastics, giving the market a warmer, earthier tone. Across town, the La Défense market, one of Europe's biggest, combines contemporary architecture with old-world festivities: skyscrapers shine overhead, while steam rises from vats of vin chaud and sizzling raclette sandwiches drip with molten cheese.

Paris have reinvented holiday luxury via taste and creativity. Angelina serves Mont-Blanc pastries topped with chestnut purée, Galette des Rois shines in boulangeries weeks before Epiphany, and Pierre Hermé's limited-edition macarons taste like spiced pear and vanilla snow. Even the air seems appetizing. When you enter Galeries Lafayette, you'll see a floating Christmas tree of glass and light hovering under the stained-glass dome, a tradition that is recreated every year in a new shape.

The ice rink of the Hôtel de Ville shines next to garland-draped great façades, while youngsters skate under fairy lights. For the season, the Eiffel Tower's observation deck has been transformed into a pop-up chalet café, providing warm mugs of mulled cider and fluffy butter croissants with a view of Paris shining underneath. And everywhere, the city hums with that distinct Parisian blend of refinement and melancholy, demonstrating that Christmas here is as much about style as it is about spirit.

2.2 Strasbourg and Alsace: the beating heart of Christmas.

In Strasbourg, even the air smells like cinnamon and clove. The cobblestones sparkle with frost, and the cathedral stands watch above kiosks selling gingerbread hearts and carved nutcrackers. Christmas is not an event here; it is a way of life that has been handed down for ages.

The Christkindelsmärik, which dates back to 1570, is Europe's oldest Christmas market, and in 2025, it seems more vibrant than ever. Instead of souvenirs, booths sell handmade fabrics, beeswax candles, and homemade bredele cookies. The city's "Green Market" project has made headlines, with solar-powered lighting, biodegradable décor, and incentives for craftsmen who use locally sourced materials. Tradition meets consciousness, shrouded in cinnamon-scented air.

A short train journey away, Colmar, Obernai, and Kaysersberg seem like fairytale drawings, with half-timbered homes covered with garlands and their reflections dancing on frozen canals. In quaint winstubs (Alsatian taverns), you may sample the region's heritage: foie gras with fig jam, steaming choucroute garnie (sauerkraut with sausages and pigs), and a drink of crisp Riesling or warming vin chaud steeped with star anise and honey.

But Alsace is more than simply nostalgia. In 2025/2026, younger craftsmen are revitalizing traditional crafts, including embroidered linen, carved wooden toys, and naturally colored jewelry. Even the Maison du Pain d'Alsace in Sélestat has started classes where you may make traditional pain d'épices (gingerbread) with local bakers. The encounter seems timeless—not a tourist display, but a view into a genuine, breathing culture.

By dusk, as the cathedral bells toll and snow starts to fall gently over the enormous Christmas tree on Place Kléber, you understand why Strasbourg proclaims itself Capitale de Noël—not out of pride, but out of love. It's a city that reminds you that Christmas was never supposed to be noisy, but rather illuminating.

2.3 Hidden Winter Escapes: Reims, Colmar, and the French Alps.

You enjoy a glass of cold Champagne while the Reims cathedral shines in delicate pink light, the bubbles rising like snowflakes. Further south, Colmar's canals reflect strings of golden stars, while in the Alps, the world is reduced to the sound of snow crunching under your feet and the promise of melting cheese over a fire. In 2025/2026, France's lesser-known winter retreats seem more personal than ever, combining festivity and peace.

In Reims, Christmas starts underground. Taittinger and Ruinart's chalk cellars provide candlelight excursions that conclude with golden glasses of vintage Champagne, each bubble whispering of centuries of craftsmanship. Above ground, the Cathédrale Notre-Dame de Reims, where French monarchs were once crowned, serves as the backdrop for a stunning light projection that transforms the Gothic façade into a narrative of winter's promise and regeneration. Around the Place d'Erlon market, you'll discover truffle-infused cheeses, mulled Champagne (yes, it exists), and warm brioches filled with praline cream. Reims in December seems like a toast—elegant, effervescent, and memorable.

Then there's **Colmar,** which is sometimes overshadowed by Strasbourg yet may be even more charming. In 2025, the town's emphasis on handcrafted authenticity gained it new status as a "Slow Christmas" destination. The six tiny marketplaces here are brimming with handcrafted toys, embroidered linens, and Alsatian ceramics – no mass manufacturing, just heart and history. The canals reflect candy-colored facades, and the air is infused with the aroma of pain d'épices and toasted almonds. Step inside L'Atelier de Yann for spiced orange hot chocolate, or take a walk to Petite Venise at night, where Christmas lights dance over the river like molten gold.

And when the mountains beckon, you respond with wool scarves and a hearty hunger. The French Alps—from Annecy's frozen lake to Chamonix's snow-dusted chalets and Megève's fairytale streets—are where Christmas becomes rustic and extravagant. In 2025, new eco-ski projects will have made it simpler to travel by train from Paris or Lyon to the Alps, with regional winter rail tickets that include savings at local lodges. At altitude, dishes focus on comfort: boiling tartiflette covered with Reblochon cheese, fondue savoyarde served with chunks of crusty bread, and raclette scraped hot into boiled potatoes and pickles.

These are more than simply meals; they are friendly rituals meant to slow down the evening and bring strangers together. Outside, snow silences the world. Inside, laughter rises alongside the steam. You understand that in France, Christmas does not need grandeur; it only requires pleasant company and something melting over the fire.

2.4 Practical Travel Insights for 2025-2026

France in December rewards the tourist who organizes like a local – trains fill up quickly, snow may halt even the most gorgeous routes, and early reservations make all the difference. However, with the perfect time and a thermos of vin chaud, you'll realize that winter here is an invitation to slow down and enjoy.

Getting around:

For now, the **SNCF *Winter Discovery Pass*** provides unrestricted regional rail travel for up to ten days on festive lines such as Paris-Strasbourg-Colmar and Lyon-Annecy-Chambéry. The new Alpine Express Line links major ski resorts directly to Geneva and Grenoble, reducing transfers and emissions. Renting a car? With France's "Noël Durable" tourist concept, many hotels and shops now provide charging stations for electric or hybrid vehicles.

Budget and Crowds:

December is peak season, particularly from December 15 to January 2. For the best deals, book in early December or the week following New Year's. Rural gîtes, vineyard B&Bs, and family-run guesthouses sometimes provide breakfast and holiday meals, adding both value and charm. Many smaller markets now demand free timed-entry passes to control crowds, so register online if feasible.

Weather and What to Pack:

Expect crisp, dry cold in the north and wetter weather in the west. Snow is dependable in Alsace and the Alps beginning in mid-December. Pack wet boots, layered thermals, and a small umbrella. Locals like stylish practicality—matching wool jackets, scarves, and gloves. Bring a tiny crossbody bag for markets and a reusable mug if you want to enjoy vin chaud responsibly (certain vendors offer discounts).

Booking and Safety Tips:

Book your market lodgings at least two months in advance, since Strasbourg, Colmar, and Paris fill up rapidly. Small booths may not take credit cards, so have cash on hand. France's public safety presence is apparent but casual; carry your ID and keep valuables handy. Most importantly, let yourself time. Winter trains may run slowly, but so does the French Christmas spirit—and that's the goal.

When you eventually stroll into a quiet cobblestone street at night, hands warm around a cup of mulled wine, you'll understand why locals say "Il faut prendre le temps de Noël" — you have to take your time with Christmas.

Chapter 3 - The French Christmas Table:

Culinary Heritage and Seasonal Rituals

3.1 The Anatomy of Réveillon

It's almost midnight, and the home smells like butter, truffles, and champagne. Outside, ice glitters on the cobblestones, but inside, the Réveillon feast has only just begun – a lengthy, opulent supper that will go until early Christmas morning. You take your seat at the table, where candles flare over cutlery and laughter echoes through the clinking of glasses. This isn't just supper. It's communion, France's method of celebrating Christmas via food, family, and tradition.

Réveillon de Noël celebrations vary throughout the nation, but the core stays consistent: plenty and camaraderie. Families assemble after midnight mass or around the fire, dressed as if for an opera, the table groaning beneath food representing area and ancestry.

- The Start: In Paris and parts of northern France, the meal begins with oysters on ice, lemon wedges, and rye bread slathered with salted butter. The brine strikes your tongue like a cool sea breeze: pure and joyous.
- The Heart: Smooth as silk foie gras appears next, either with fig jam or a sprinkle of Sauternes. In the Loire Valley, it might be substituted with smoked eel, while in Brittany, lobster fried in garlic butter.
- The centerpiece of the feast may be chapon rôti (roast chicken), dinde aux marrons (chestnut-stuffed turkey), or boeuf en croûte (beef Wellington). The air thickens with thyme, roasting fat, and wine reduction scents.
- Finally, there's the bûche de Noël, a pastry version of the Yule log. Each location makes it differently: praline in Lyon, chestnut cream in Paris, and citrus mousse in the Riviera.

Modern *Réveillons* in 2025 demonstrate a minor change. Younger families are combining plant-forward diets with traditional dishes, such as mushroom pâté in place of foie gras and local sparkling cider in place of Champagne. Sustainability is no longer a statement; rather, it is a gentle grace note at the table. Nonetheless, the ceremony continues — candles burn low, someone pours the last of the wine, and laughter echoes into the night. You understand that Christmas in France is about unwrapping moments rather than goods.

3.2 Regional Holiday Specialties

Traveling over France during Christmas is like eating an atlas of memory: each area has its own taste, and each dish tells a narrative. By the time you traverse the nation, your taste buds will have traveled through centuries of culinary tradition.

Alsace—Spice, Sweetness, and Germanic Soul

You can taste Christmas in the air here. The aroma of pain d'épices (spiced gingerbread) and mulled wine accompanies you through the market booths.

- Signature delicacies include choucroute garnie (sauerkraut with pork and sausages), foie gras d'Alsace, and bredele cookies.
- Where to eat it: At Maison Kammerzell near Strasbourg Cathedral, order choucroute royale while the Christmas tree lights reflect off the Rhine.

Brittany—Sea, Butter, and Tradition

The Atlantic breeze brings salt into the kitchens of Brittany. Christmas Eve here is simple, coastal, and full of flavor.

- Signature dishes include homard à l'armoricaine (lobster in tomato-cognac sauce), galettes de blé noir (buckwheat crêpes), and butter-soaked kouign-amann for dessert.

- In 2025, local co-ops will host "Fishermen's Christmas" feasts in Saint-Malo and Concarneau, with fresh catch dishes and storytelling by retired seamen.

Provence – Light, Faith, and the 13 Desserts

In Provence, the emphasis is on elegance rather than grandeur while celebrating. After midnight mass, tables are adorned with Les Treize Desserts, a symbolic dish honoring Christ and the apostles.

- Signature meals include aïoli de morue (salted fish with garlic sauce), pompe à l'huile (olive oil bread), and calissons d'Aix (figs, almonds, and nougat).
- Where to go: Beginning in 2025, the Avignon "Route des Treize Desserts" will allow visitors to enjoy sweets from ancient patisseries and convent bakeries.

Burgundy—Wine, Earth, and Indulgence

Christmas starts and finishes in the vineyard.

- Signature dishes include coq au vin, œufs en meurette (poached eggs in red wine sauce), and bœuf bourguignon slow-cooked in Pinot Noir.

- In December, several wineries offer "Vignerons de Noël" weekends, which include candlelight tastings, handmade gingerbread, and truffle cheese.

Savoy and the Alps—Fire, Snow, and Comfort

Dinner in the mountain chalets represents both survival and delight. Snow falls thickly outside; within, everything melts.

- Signature meals include tartiflette, raclette, Savoyard fondue, and diots au vin blanc (white wine sausages).
- Experience tip: The Annecy Winter Market 2025 has launched "Fromage Fridays," during which local dairies demonstrate cheese-making and offer community fondues by the lake.

Every meal teaches you something new about the area, the people, and the changing seasons. By the time you leave

France, you'll learn that Christmas is all about savoring —
each sip of wine, each crumb of cake, and each tale shared
between meals.

3.3 The Art of French Festive Dining.

You don't have to live in Paris to eat like the French at
Christmas; all you need is to recognize that the dinner is a
ritual rather than a hurry. The French celebratory meal is
about mood rather than plenty, with light, texture, and
laughing as important as butter and wine.

Imagine your table shimmering with the subtle flicker of
candles. Linen napkins are folded into fans and nestled with
a sprig of rosemary. Porcelain dishes shine under crystal
glasses, while in the background, Charles Aznavour hums
quietly from a vintage playlist. This is Noël à la
française—timeless but vibrant, beautiful but never rigid.

To prepare your French festive table:
- Colors: Choose warm whites, forest greens, and a
  dash of gold to reflect both the snowy Alps and the
  sparkle of Parisian lights.

- Textures: Combine rustic and elegant elements, such as polished silver with handmade ceramics or linen runners on top of hardwood tables.
- Aroma: A tiny dish of cloves and orange peels cooking close quickly evokes nostalgia.

Wine pairings and toasts:

- Begin with Champagne or Crémant d'Alsace, a crisp and joyful French icon of joie de vivre.
- Pour a chilled Muscadet or Chablis with oysters or other seafood appetizers.
- The main dish, which is usually capon, duck, or venison, calls for a full-bodied Burgundy Pinot Noir or Bordeaux mix.

- Sauternes complements sweet pastries, while sparkling rosé pairs well with Bûche de Noël.

Etiquette for Your Réveillon Table:
- The host always initiates the toast by lifting their glass with "Joyeux Noël à tous!" before others join.
- Bread is put directly on the tablecloth rather than on a side dish, which is a modest but striking French touch.
- Cheese comes after the main course, not before it, and coffee is always served after dessert, never with it.

Creating this experience at home does not need perfection. It's about enjoying conversation as flavorful as the sauce, laughter that lingers like the aroma of vanilla and butter. In France, dining well at Christmas means living well, even if just for one magical night.

3.4 Market to Table Traditions

If you want to cook like the French for Christmas, start where they do: at the market before daybreak. The weather is frigid enough to turn your breath into smoke, yet the stalls are vibrant with color, perfume, and bustle. This is where

Christmas actually begins: under striped awnings, with a wicker basket on your arm and a warm croissant in hand.

You go by tables of shiny chestnuts, truffled cheeses, and ruby-red cranberries that shine like diamonds in the winter light. The fishmonger announces the morning's catch, which includes baskets of Belon oysters, langoustines, and Normandy sea scallops sparkling on ice. Nearby, a baker prepares golden brioche coated with pearl sugar, their perfume wafting into the crisp air like a warm promise.

An authentic French Christmas market list may include:

- Oysters (huîtres): Purchased fresh and served raw with shallot vinegar or lemon – the glory of Christmas Eve settings.
- Foie gras is a luxury delicacy that is either created at home or acquired from reputable craftsmen in the Southwest.
- Cheese board basics include Brie de Meaux, Comté, Roquefort, and a tart goat cheese from the Loire Valley.
- Seasonal veggies include leeks, celeriac, chestnuts, and baby carrots, which are modest elements elevated to grandeur.

- Bread and pastries include baguettes for dinner, pain d'épices (spiced bread) for dessert, and Bûche de Noël from your local pâtisserie.

By 10 a.m., the markets are crowded, with youngsters clutching hot chocolate cups and their parents debating the finest Champagne vintage for the family toast. In tiny towns, grandmothers still bundle fresh herbs for roasting, while in major cities, fashionable eco-markets offer organic turkeys and plant-based pâtés as a new take on tradition.

Practical Tip: In 2025/2026, France's local markets will emphasize sustainability via recyclable containers, regional food, and seasonal awareness. Travelers may also attend Christmas cooking lessons in Alsace or Provence to learn how to transform market discoveries into festive feasts.

By the time you get home, your basket is full, but your heart is light. The markets are more than simply places to purchase food; they're a celebration of community. The farmer, the baker, and the fromager have all contributed something unique to your Christmas table.

And when the candles are lighted that evening, each mouthful tells a tale of frost-covered mornings, long walks through cobblestone neighborhoods, and the delight that can only come from something produced, shared, and relished together.

Chapter 4 - Festive Recipes from France

Classics and Hidden Gems
(A culinary journey through France's most beloved Christmas dishes—where narrative meets kitchen magic.)

4.1 Starters and Warm Beginnings.

When the first fragrance of roasted chestnuts fills the air and markets are thronged with oysters, truffles, and winter herbs, you know it's Christmastime in France. A French Noël supper begins with subtle preludes that excite the senses and set the tone for the feast to come. They express not just taste, but also tradition—the French art of savoring the season with love, generosity, and elegance.

Huîtres Gratinees: Gratinated oysters with Champagne cream.

The French like oysters at Christmas, whether raw, fresh, or served up in elegance. By 2025, many Parisian households will be sourcing from eco-farms in Brittany or Normandy, embracing sustainability without sacrificing shine. Imagine yourself in a candlelit kitchen, spooning rich Champagne cream over plump oysters, the saline scent blending with shallots and butter.

Why is it on the table?

Because oysters are the flavor of Christmas Eve in France, combining luxury and simplicity, linking the sea and revelry.

Typical Market Findings:

- Fresh oysters from Cancale or Arcachon.
- Shallots, butter, Champagne, and a splash of cream.
- Fresh parsley and breadcrumbs for texture.

🍄 Soup with Truffle Mushrooms

As frost covers the roofs, French kitchens fill with the earthy aroma of mushrooms. In Alsace and the Loire, families prepare velouté, a creamy, silky soup that feels like a warm embrace on a chilly evening. The addition of seasonal truffles transforms it into a Christmas treasure.

Why is it on the table?

It epitomizes French comfort and elegance, with basic ingredients transformed into magnificent dishes through time and care.

Sensory Scene:

You stir gently, the wooden spoon making languid circles through the steam. Outside, bells ring out from the town square, while inside, the perfume of thyme and garlic fills the air.

Typical Market Findings:

- Wild mushrooms, truffles, and shallots
- Cream, butter, thyme, and a dash of cognac

Fine tart with goat cheese and honey.

In Provence, where the Christmas lights last longer, holiday starts are rustic and golden. This delicate tart combines creamy chèvre, wildflower honey, and a drizzle of olive oil for the ideal mix of sweetness and acidity.

Why is it on the table?

It connects areas, from the goat farms of the Loire Valley to the lavender fields of Provence, reminding every French table that Christmas is both personal and communal.

Typical Market Findings:

- Chèvre cheese, acacia honey, and puff pastry.
- Thyme, walnuts, with a dash of black pepper.

🍃 Winter Vegetable Terrine.

An allusion to the rising 2025 trend of plant-based eating. This vibrant terrine, made with roasted carrots, beets, and leeks covered with herbed goat cheese and pistachios, can be found at eco-conscious Parisian bistros.

Why is it on the table:

Because French tradition develops, it respects the environment while maintaining taste at its core.

Typical Market Findings:

- Seasonal root veggies.
- Goat cheese or mascarpone, olive oil, and herbs de Provence.

4.2 Main Courses for Celebration.

French Christmas dinners are balanced feasts that are both sumptuous and elegant, based on tradition yet open to new ideas. Whether it's the golden crackling of roasted duck or the rich, wine-soaked scent of coq au vin simmering on the stove, each meal tells a tale about family, place, and custom.

🦆 Duck in Orange Glaze

This meal, once a royal favorite at Versailles, now adorns Christmas tables across France, its rich perfume filling dining rooms as songs waft from adjacent churches. The glossy sauce, which is a combination of fresh orange juice, caramel, and stock, elevates the soft duck to new heights of taste and texture.

Why is it on the table?

It exemplifies French culinary finesse, mixing richness with brightness, history, and delight.

Sensory Scene:

You baste the duck until the skin becomes caramel and crisp, with citrus zest dancing in the air. The glaze thickens, sweet and acidic, while laughing fills the adjacent room.

Key Ingredients:

- Duck, fresh oranges, sugar, vinegar, chicken broth, and butter
- Orange zest, thyme, and a dash of Grand Marnier

🍷 Bourgogne-Style Chicken with Red Wine

This classic recipe, which originated in the vineyards of Burgundy, tastes like French winter in a pot. It is traditionally cooked for hours in red wine, mushrooms, onions, and lardons, exemplifying patience — the French method of cooking with heart rather than hurry.

Why is it on the table?

Because it's a meal that draws everyone together: family gathering around, sharing from the same pot, relishing the richness of wine and tradition.

Sensory Scene:

The sauce quietly bubbles, infusing the kitchen with the aroma of thyme, garlic, and wine-soaked warmth. Every mouthful is soft, deep, and memorable.

Key Ingredients:

- Chicken, red Burgundy wine, bacon lardons, mushrooms, and pearl onions
- thyme, bay leaf, garlic, and butter.

Tartiflette Savoyarde (Alpine Cheese Potato Gratin).

In the snow-covered Alpine villages of Annecy and Megève, tartiflette is both a meal and a memory. Layers of potatoes, reblochon cheese, onions, and bacon bake gently until bubbling—the type of meal that feels like returning home after a day on the slopes.

Why is it on the table?

Because no French winter feast is complete without comforting food that melts on your tongue and warms your spirit.

Typical Market Findings:

- Reblochon cheese, potatoes, onions, smoky bacon, and crème fraîche.

🦃 Roasted capon with chestnuts

A French Christmas isn't complete without chapon, a delicate, slow-roasted capon served with chestnut stuffing and thick pan juices. In 2025, many families will prefer organic or farm-raised chickens, combining tradition and sustainability.

Why is it on the table:

Because it's the focal point—the moment when quiet falls, glasses are raised, and all that remains is the perfume of roasted perfection.

Sensory Scene:

Steam rises from the dish as you slice. The skin is golden and crunchy; the chestnut filling is soft and sweet, seasoned with butter and spices.

Key Ingredients:

- Capon or big chicken, chestnuts, butter, herbs, bread, cream, and white wine.

✦ *Practical tip for 2025/2026:*

More French chefs are adopting regional fusion, such as offering Duck à l'Orange with Provençal herbs or matching Tartiflette with Champagne rather than white wine. Modern bistros like Lyon, Annecy, and Paris's 9th arrondissement provide travelers with a direct encounter with these inventive twists.

4.3 Sides, Sauces, and Seasonal Pairings

A great French Christmas meal is never just about the main course; it's the symphony of sides and sauces that make each mouthful sing. Each texture is deliberate: the smooth whisper of puréed celery root against the crisp saltiness of roasted potatoes; the tang of red wine reduction to balance the richness of duck. In France, sides are more than just afterthoughts; they are subtle works of culinary poetry.

Dauphinois (Creamy Potato Gratin)

There's a reason why this meal has become a favorite at every French Christmas table. Thinly sliced potatoes drenched in cream, garlic, and nutmeg, roasted till brown and bubbling—it's simplicity converted into indulgence. In 2025, many French chefs will add Comté or Gruyère for a nutty flavor.

Texture and Harmony:
- Creamy: The cooked cream embraces each potato layer.
- Crisp: The top develops a golden crust that shatters with a fork.
- Earthy: Nutmeg and garlic balance the richness.

Pair with duck à l'orange, roasted capon, or mushroom velouté for a vegetarian meal.

🫛 Green Beans with Garlic and Butter.

Every French meal needs something fresh and green to counterbalance the butter and wine. These thin green beans, delicately sautéed with garlic and butter, offer the necessary crispness and brightness to the meal.

Why this matters:

- Because, despite their excess, the French understand moderation – a dish that cleanses the palette while framing the rest in harmony.

2025 Market Tip:

- Look for winter-harvested beans from Provence, which are smaller, sweeter, and perfect for rapid pan-cooking.

Sauce du Vin rouge (Red Wine Sauce)

This sauce, which serves as the foundation for many French roasts, adds richness and complexity to any holiday meal. A reduction of Burgundy wine, shallots, butter, and veal stock—it's where patience turns simple into luxury.

Flavor Profile:

- Deep and velvety: Wine and stock provide a rich basis.

- Aromatic: Shallots and thyme provide aroma and structure.
- Balanced: Finish with a bit of butter to smooth off any rough edges.

Pairs well with coq au vin, beef tenderloin, and roasted duck.

⬤ Celery Root Purée

This recipe spans the gap between rustic and elegant in Michelin kitchens as well as rural houses. It's somewhat nutty and airy flavor complements powerful meats and rich sauces without dominating them.

Why the French adore it:

- Because it feels luxurious yet light – a classy alternative to mashed potatoes that is often drizzled with truffle oil or served with toasted hazelnuts.

Sensory snapshot:

- A spoonful dissolves on your tongue, its silkiness accompanied by a delicate scent of truffle and cream.

4.4 Dessert, Treats, and Drinks

If French Christmas has a pulse, it's in its sweets, which combine memory and skill. Every confection has a story: monks in Burgundy baking honeyed spice bread, Parisian pâtissiers rolling cakes into logs, and youngsters laughing as powdered sugar dusts their noses. Dessert in France is more than simply something to eat; it is something to be celebrated and enjoyed.

◆ Yule Log Cake (Bûche de Noël).

This rolling sponge cake, which originated as an old Yule log ritual, has become the centerpiece of every French Christmas dinner. In 2025, pâtisseries in Paris offer everything from chestnut cream and dark chocolate to vegan praline variations, but the tradition stays the same: slicing into its creamy spirals as family gathers around.

Story and Symbolism:

The original Yule log burned on the winter solstice, representing warmth and rebirth. Today's edible version — buttercream and ganache — keeps the flame alive.

Texture Symphony:

- Soft genoise sponge.
- Silky cream or mousse.
- Dusting with powdered sugar "snow"

Tips for Home Bakers:

- While the cake is still warm, roll it with a clean dish towel to keep the sponge pliable and avoid breaking.

👑 Galette des Rois (King's Cake)

Although it is officially associated with January's Epiphany, Galette des Rois, a golden, flaky pastry filled with almond frangipane, is often seen in December windows. The fève (a little charm) is hidden within, and the person who discovers it becomes "king" or "queen" for the day.

A Slice of Culture:

It's not just dessert; it's theater. Families crown one another, laughing as the youngest kid hides beneath the table to distribute slices "fairly."

- Bakeries in Lyon and Bordeaux are now producing sustainable galettes with fair-trade almonds and biodegradable crowns.

Key Ingredients:

- Puff pastry, almond cream (frangipane), and egg yolk glaze

🍞 Pain d'Épices (French Spiced Honey Bread)

This is France's version of gingerbread, warm and dark, with notes of cinnamon, orange zest, and cloves. In Dijon, it is still produced the old-fashioned method, using rye flour and aged honey. The outcome is thick yet soft, perfect with a glass of vin chaud.

Why It Endures:

- Because it evokes memories of hearths, children, and the aroma of winter markets long after they have closed.
- Pair with foie gras, mulled wine, or simply buttered toast for breakfast.

Vin Chaud (French Mulled Wine)

Every Christmas market from Strasbourg to Nice has hands wrapped around steamy mugs of vin chaud. Each area has its own secret - Alsace uses white wine and star anise, while Lyon swears by red Burgundy and orange peel.

Sensory Description:

You lift the cup and inhale, smelling cloves, citrus, and red wine in the frigid air. One sip and your breath is filled with spice and warmth.

How To Make It (The French Way):

- One bottle of red wine (Bordeaux or Côtes du Rhône).
- 1 orange, zested and sliced
- 4 cloves, 1 cinnamon stick, and 2 tablespoons sugar.
- Heat slowly but never boil, and serve steaming.

✨ *2025/2026 Dessert Trends:*

French pastry chefs are recreating classics with botanical tastes, such as lavender praline logs, rosemary-infused galettes, and vin chaud created with organic cider. Dessert bars in Paris now offer "Noël Tasting Flights," which match small Bûches with local dessert wines such as Sauternes and Banyuls.

Chapter 5: "Bringing France Home

Celebrate a French Christmas Anywhere"

This chapter will help you recreate the warmth and enchantment of a French Noël wherever you are, from the brightness of Parisian cafés to the comfortable clink of wine glasses at a family table.

5.1 Setting the French Christmas Mood at Home

Close your eyes and envision this: it's Christmas Eve, and your house is filled with the mellow amber light of candles flickering amid evergreen garlands. The perfume of spiced wine, orange peel, and vanilla sugar fills the air, reminiscent of a French Noël. You may be thousands of miles away from Paris, but tonight, you will bring the same joie de vivre into your own house.

In France, ambiance is as important as the cuisine itself. To create that unique French Christmas atmosphere:

- **Set the tone with scent:**
  Light candles infused with *cinnamon, clove, and pine*, or simmer a small pot of *mulled wine* with orange zest and star anise on the stove. In Provence,

families still use dried lavender sachets tied with red ribbons — a subtle floral note that whispers of the French countryside even in winter.

- **Decorate with understated elegance:**

    Think natural textures — *linen napkins, wooden chargers, sprigs of rosemary*, and soft golden fairy lights woven through a simple centerpiece of pinecones and citrus. The French Christmas table is not about extravagance, but refinement. It's the kind of beauty that feels effortless.

- **Music that warms the spirit:**

    Create a playlist blending *classic French carols* like "Il est né, le divin Enfant" with gentle jazz renditions of Noël standards. In Parisian homes, it's common to hear Charles Aznavour or Carla Bruni softly in the background as glasses are raised.

- **The rhythm of the evening:**
  The French never rush a meal. A true *Réveillon de Noël* unfolds slowly — starting with an apéritif, followed by conversation, and each dish served with intention. As you host, take cues from that rhythm: dim the lights, linger between courses, and let the evening become its own story.

By the time dessert comes, you'll have experienced the distinct combination of warmth, laughter, and satisfaction that distinguishes a French Christmas. You'll discover that it's about mood rather than geography. You have caught France right where you are.

5.2 A Paris-Inspired Holiday Menu Plan

Now that your house resembles the center of Paris in December, it's time to prepare a feast worthy of its radiance. Let's create a Parisian Christmas soirée that is both exquisite and doable, catering to people who want authenticity without being intimidated.

Here are two full meal ideas, one classic and one contemporary, designed for 2025's celebratory tables:

Menu 1: The Classic Parisian Noël (5 Courses)

A menu that could grace a Haussmann apartment overlooking the Seine — timeless, indulgent, and deeply French.

1. Apéritif: *Kir Royal* — Champagne with a dash of crème de cassis, served with *gougères* (warm cheese puffs)
   - *Tip:* Bake gougères ahead of time and reheat briefly before guests arrive.
2. Entrée (Starter): *Foie gras au torchon* with fig compote and toasted brioche
   - *Pair with:* A glass of *Sauternes* or *Jurançon doux* — its honeyed notes complement the richness perfectly.
3. Plat principal (Main): *Canard à l'orange* (Roast duck with orange glaze) served with *gratin dauphinois* and buttered green beans
   - *Chef's Note:* Rest the duck for 15 minutes before carving — patience makes perfection.
4. Fromage (Cheese course): A trio of French cheeses — *Comté, Brie de Meaux, and Roquefort* — with walnut bread and pear slices

- *Pair with:* A medium-bodied *Burgundy Pinot Noir.*

5. Dessert: *Bûche de Noël au chocolat et marron* — a traditional yule log with chocolate ganache and chestnut cream

   - *Serve with:* A shot of espresso or *Cognac* for a sophisticated finale.

🍴 **Menu 2: The Modern Parisian Table (3 courses)**

A refined but quicker alternative for smaller gatherings — perfect for 2025's fast-paced hosts who still want that French flair.

1. Starter: *Velouté de potimarron* (Creamy pumpkin soup) with a drizzle of truffle oil and toasted hazelnuts
   - *Tip:* Make it a day ahead — the flavors deepen overnight.
2. Main: *Filet de sole meunière* (pan-seared sole with lemon butter sauce) served with *roasted winter vegetables*
   - *Pair with:* A chilled *Chablis* or *Alsace Riesling.*
3. Dessert: *Tarte Tatin* with vanilla ice cream or *Madeleines* dusted with powdered sugar
   - *Finish with:* A festive *vin chaud* (mulled wine) scented with cinnamon and orange peel.

Timing Tips for Your Parisian Soirée:

- Two days before: Prepare desserts, sauces, and dressings.
- Morning of: Set the table and pre-chop vegetables.
- One hour before: Warm plates in a low oven — a French secret for restaurant-level presentation.
- During the meal: Pour wine in small, frequent servings to keep conversation flowing naturally.

And remember — a French Christmas meal is never about perfection. It's about *presence*. As your guests lean back, smiling between bites, and the last notes of your holiday playlist fade, you'll feel it: the same magic that fills the brasseries of Paris every December.

You haven't just cooked a meal. You've hosted a moment — one that sparkles with *la magie de Noël à la française*

5.3 Gift, Tradition, and Hosting Tips

If there is one thing the French understand well, it is mindfulness. At Christmas, every gesture has importance, from the way a bottle of wine is wrapped to the ribbon tied around a handmade jam. Gifting in France is not about grandeur or price. It's all about aim and taste.

Consider yourself in a little village in Alsace on Christmas Eve. The air smells of roasted chestnuts and pain d'épices, as families rush home with armfuls of nicely wrapped presents. Each has a tale - a reflection of friendship and tradition. You can bring the same love and caring into your house, no matter where you are.

Here's how the French do it — and how you can, too:

- Edible Gifts from the Heart:
  A French Christmas gift often begins in the kitchen. Think *homemade truffles rolled in cocoa powder*, jars of *salted caramel*, or *candied orange peels dipped in dark chocolate*. For something regional, recreate:
    - *Calissons d'Aix* (almond-shaped marzipan sweets from Provence)
    - *Nougat de Montélimar* wrapped in parchment

- *Sablés de Noël* (buttery Christmas cookies from Normandy) tied with red twine
  Each tells a story — a flavor from somewhere special.
- The Art of Presentation:
  French gifts are rarely overwrapped or ostentatious. Instead, they're beautifully simple: brown kraft paper, natural twine, and a small sprig of rosemary or dried orange slice tucked beneath the bow. A handwritten tag saying *"Avec toute mon affection"* (With all my affection) adds the final touch of sincerity.
- Handwritten Cards Still Matter:
  In an increasingly digital world, handwritten notes remain sacred in France. A *carte de vœux* (holiday card) is usually written with care, expressing warmth rather than formality. Phrases like *"Joyeux Noël et Bonne Année — que la saison vous apporte bonheur et lumière"* ("Merry Christmas and Happy New Year — may the season bring you happiness and light") are common and heartfelt.
- Hosting, à la Française:
  The French host with *ease and rhythm*, not perfection. A good host ensures the table is beautifully set — perhaps with mismatched but

charming plates, a bottle of *Bordeaux breathing quietly on the counter*, and a dessert already chilling. The magic lies in pacing: conversation flows, the candles burn low, and the evening feels like a shared secret between friends.

- For Global Readers:
  Bring a touch of French charm to your own gifting by focusing on *connection over cost*. Bake a regional treat, write a note in your own handwriting, or curate a small "taste of France" box — a wedge of Comté, a jar of Dijon mustard, a bar of Valrhona chocolate. The message is simple: *I thought of you with care.*

In France, Christmas isn't just an event. It's a feeling — one you give away, piece by piece, through scent, flavor, and sincerity.

5.4 Happy Holidays in French

Raise your glass, whether it's champagne from Reims, mulled wine from Strasbourg, or a simple Bordeaux enjoyed with friends. Let us drink to what France teaches us about Christmas: joy is radiant, not loud; it is found in the grace with which we share what we have.

You've explored the glistening marketplaces of Alsace, warmed your hands around steamy cups of vin chaud, and sampled your way through bistros and bakeries where the air smells of butter and promise. You've found that every French cuisine has a tale about family, tradition, and the peaceful enchantment of a winter evening.

Take a minute when the lights are flickering and the final crumbs of Bûche de Noël lie on the dish. Listen. The midnight bells are ringing somewhere in a winter country or a metropolitan plaza, and people all across France are gathering around tables, smiling, sharing, and remembering.

This is the genuine heart of Noël à la française.

- Laughter fills a kitchen at twilight.
- The delight of giving a handmade present.
- The flavor of a meal shared leisurely and without haste.
- Knowing that beauty may be found in the smallest of details brings peace.

So, wherever this book finds you—whether beneath the brilliant lights of Paris or in your own snug house hundreds of miles away—may your season be filled with warmth, wonder, and connection.

Joyeux Noël et Bonne Année —

From our French table to yours, with love and light.

Printed in Dunstable, United Kingdom